DEDICATION

I humbly dedicate this work to the supreme spiritual being.

CHAPTER 1

INTRODUCTION TO C# PROGRAMMING

Welcome to the world of C# programming! This chapter will provide you with an introduction to C# and why it is an essential language to learn. You will also learn how to set up the development environment and write and run your first program. Let's get started!

WHAT IS C#?

C# (pronounced "C sharp") is a modern, high-level programming language designed for developing software applications for Microsoft's .NET platform. It was first introduced in 2000 and has since become one of the most popular programming languages in the world. C# is used for a wide variety of applications, including desktop applications, web applications, mobile apps, video games, and more.

WHY LEARN C#?

Learning C# provides many benefits, including:

1. **Wide Range of Applications**: C# is used for a wide range of applications, including desktop and web

applications, games, and mobile apps. It is also used for developing software for the Microsoft Windows operating system.

2. **High Demand**: C# is one of the most popular programming languages, and there is a high demand for developers with C# skills.

3. **Easy to Learn**: C# is an easy to learn language, making it an excellent choice for beginners.

4. **Object-Oriented Programming (OOP):** C# is an object-oriented language, which means it allows you to create reusable code and organize your code into logical classes and objects.

5. **Great Community Support**: C# has a vast community of developers who provide support and share their knowledge through online forums and communities.

SETTING UP THE DEVELOPMENT ENVIRONMENT

To start developing C# programs, you will need to set up your development environment. Here are the steps you need to follow:

1. Download and Install Visual Studio: Visual Studio is the most popular development environment for C# programming. You can download the free Visual Studio Community Edition from the Microsoft website.

2. Create a New Project: Once you have installed Visual Studio, you can create a new C# project. To do this, open Visual Studio, select "File" > "New" > "Project", and then select "Console Application" from the list of project templates.

3. Write Your Code: Once you have created your project, you can start writing your code. You will write your code in the "Program.cs" file that is automatically created for you.

WRITING AND RUNNING YOUR FIRST PROGRAM

Now that you have set up your development environment, it is time to write and run your first C# program. *Here is an example program that prints "Hello, World!" to the console:*

```csharp
using System;

namespace HelloWorld
{
    class Program
    {
        static void Main(string[] args)
        {
            Console.WriteLine("Hello, World!");
        }
    }
}
```

Let's break down the code:

- **using System;**: This line tells the compiler to use the "System" namespace, which contains the Console class that we will use to print to the console.

- **namespace HelloWorld**: This line creates a namespace called "HelloWorld" to contain our program.

- **class Program**: This line defines a class called "Program" that contains our program's code.

- **static void Main(string[] args)**: This line defines the main method of our program, which is the entry point for the program.

- **Console.WriteLine("Hello, World!");**: This line prints "Hello, World!" to the console.

To run your program, you can click the "Start" button in Visual Studio, or you can press "F5" on your keyboard. You should see "Hello, World!" printed on the console.

EXERCISE:

1. Write a program that asks the user for their name and then prints it "

CHAPTER 2

VARIABLES AND DATA TYPES

In this chapter, we will discuss variables and data types in C#. These are fundamental concepts in programming that allow you to store and manipulate data in your programs.

WHAT ARE VARIABLES?

Variables are containers that hold data or values that can be used in your program. They are named locations in memory that store values of different data types. Variables can be changed during program execution and are used to hold values for calculations, comparisons, and data storage.

DECLARING AND INITIALIZING

Variables Before you can use a variable in your program, you must declare it. Declaring a variable is the process of reserving space in memory for that variable. You must specify the data type of the variable you are declaring.

Here is an example of declaring a variable of type integer named "myNumber":

```
int myNumber;
```

In this example, we declare a variable called "myNumber" of type integer. The integer data type stores whole numbers such as -1, 0, 1, 2, 3, etc.

Once you have declared a variable, you can initialize it with a value. Initializing a variable is the process of assigning an initial value to the variable.

Here is an example of declaring and initializing a variable of type string named "myName":

```
string myName = "John";
```

In this example, we declare a variable called "myName" of type *string* and initialize it with the value "John". The string data type stores text values such as "Hello", "World", etc.

COMMON DATA TYPES IN C#

C# supports several data types, each with its own set of values and operations. Here are some common data types in C#:

- **int**: stores whole numbers, such as -1, 0, 1, 2, 3, etc.

- **double**: stores floating-point numbers, such as 3.14, 5.5, 100.0, etc.

- **bool**: stores true/false values, such as true or false.

- **string**: stores text values, such as "Hello", "World", etc.

- **char**: stores single characters, such as 'a', 'b', 'c', etc.

Here are some examples of declaring and initializing variables of different data types:

```
int myAge = 30;
double mySalary = 50000.0;
bool isStudent = true;
string myName = "John";
char firstInitial = 'J';
```

EXERCISE:

1. Declare and initialize a variable of type string named "**favoriteColor**" with your favorite color.

2. Print the value of the variable to the console.

CHAPTER 3

OPERATORS AND EXPRESSIONS

In programming, operators are used to perform operations on data. Operators can be used to perform arithmetic, comparison, and logical operations. Expressions are combinations of operators and values that produce a result.

ARITHMETIC OPERATORS

Arithmetic operators are used to perform mathematical operations on numerical data. *Here are some of the most common arithmetic operators in C#:*

1. **Addition (+):** Adds two values together. *Example:*

```
int sum = 5 + 10;
```

2. **Subtraction (-):** Subtracts one value from another. *Example:*

```
int difference = 10 - 5;
```

3. **Multiplication (*):** Multiplies two values together. *Example:*

```
int product = 5 * 10;
```

4. **Division (/):** Divides one value by another. *Example:*

```
int quotient = 10 / 5;
```

5. **Modulus (%):** Returns the remainder of a division operation. *Example:*

```
int remainder = 10 % 3; // remainder = 1
```

Comparison operators are used to compare two values and return a Boolean (true/false) result. *Here are some of the most common comparison operators in C#:*

1. **Equal to (==):** Returns true if two values are equal. *Example:*

```
bool isEqual = 5 == 5; // isEqual = true
```

2. **Not equal to (!=):** Returns true if two values are not equal. *Example:*

```
bool isNotEqual = 5 != 10; // isNotEqual = true
```

3. **Greater than (>):** Returns true if one value is greater than another. *Example:*

```
bool isGreaterThan = 10 > 5; // isGreaterThan = true
```

4. **Less than (<):** Returns true if one value is less than another. *Example:*

```
bool isLessThan = 5 < 10; // isLessThan = true
```

5. **Greater than or equal to (>=):** Returns true if one value is greater than or equal to another. *Example:*

```
bool isGreaterThanOrEqual = 10 >= 5; // isGreaterThanOrEqual = true
```

6. **Less than or equal to (<=):** Returns true if one value is less than or equal to another. *Example:*

```
bool isLessThanOrEqual = 5 <= 10; // isLessThanOrEqual = true
```

LOGICAL OPERATORS

Logical operators are used to combine multiple boolean values and return a boolean result. Here are some of the most common logical operators in C#:

1. **AND (&&):** Returns true if both values are true. *Example:*

```
bool isTrue = true && true; // isTrue = true
```

2. **OR (||):** Returns true if either value is true. *Example:*

```
bool isTrue = true || false; // isTrue = true
```

3. **NOT (!):** Returns the opposite of a boolean value. *Example:*

```
bool isTrue = !false; // isTrue = true
```

UNDERSTANDING EXPRESSIONS

An expression is a combination of values and operators that produce a result. In C#, expressions can be used in many places, such as in assignment statements, function calls, and conditional statements.

For example:

```
int result = (5 + 10) * 2; // result = 30
```

In this example, the expression **(5 + 10) * 2** is evaluated to produce the value 30, which is then assigned to the variable **result**.

1. Write a program that asks the user for their age and checks if they are eligible to vote (age >= 18).

CHAPTER 4

CONTROL STRUCTURES

Control structures are used in programming to control the flow of execution of a program. They allow the program to make decisions based on certain conditions or repeat a block of code multiple times. In this chapter, we will cover some of the most used control structures in C#: If statements, switch statements, and loops.

IF STATEMENTS

An *if statement* is a decision-making statement in C# that allows the program to execute certain statements based on a particular condition. *The syntax of an if statement is as follows:*

```
if (condition)
{
    // code to execute if condition is true
}
```

Here, **condition** is the expression that is evaluated to either true or false. If the condition is true, the code inside the curly braces will be executed. If the condition is false, the code will be skipped.

For example, let's say we want to write a program that checks if a number is even or odd:

```
int number = 10;

if (number % 2 == 0)
{
    Console.WriteLine(number + " is even");
}
else
{
    Console.WriteLine(number + " is odd");
}
```

In this example, we first declare and initialize a variable **number** with the value 10. We then use an *if statement* to check if **number** is even or odd. The expression **number % 2 == 0** checks if the remainder of **number** divided by 2 is equal to 0. If it is, the number is even, and the first **Console.WriteLine** statement will execute. If it is not, the number is odd, and the second **Console.WriteLine** statement will execute.

SWITCH STATEMENTS

A switch statement is another decision-making statement that allows the program to execute different sections of code depending on the value of a variable. *The syntax of a switch statement is as follows:*

```
switch (expression)
{
    case value1:
        // code to execute if expression equals value1
        break;
    case value2:
        // code to execute if expression equals value2
        break;
    // more cases here
    default:
        // code to execute if expression does not equal any of the values
        break;
}
```

Here, **expression** is the variable that is being checked, and **value1**, **value2**, etc. are the values that it could equal. The **break** statement is used to exit the switch statement once a matching case has been found. If none of the cases match, the code inside the **default** block will be executed.

For example, let's say we want to write a program that displays a message based on the day of the week:

```
string dayOfWeek = "Monday";

switch (dayOfWeek)
{
    case "Monday":
        Console.WriteLine("Today is Monday");
        break;
    case "Tuesday":
        Console.WriteLine("Today is Tuesday");
        break;
    case "Wednesday":
        Console.WriteLine("Today is Wednesday");
        break;
    case "Thursday":
        Console.WriteLine("Today is Thursday");
        break;
    case "Friday":
        Console.WriteLine("Today is Friday");
        break;
    default:
        Console.WriteLine("It's the weekend!");
        break;
}
```

In this example, we declare and initialize a variable **dayOfWeek** with the value "Monday". We then use a switch statement to display a message based on the value of **dayOfWeek**. Since **dayOfWeek** is "Monday", the first case matches and the program displays the message "Today is Monday".

Loops are used to execute a block of code multiple times. There are three types of loops in C#: while loops, do-while loops, and for loops.

A *while loop* allows you to repeatedly execute a block of code if a certain condition is true.

The basic structure of a while loop is as follows:

```
while (condition)
{
    // block of code to be executed
}
```

The **condition** in the *while loop* is a Boolean expression that determines whether the loop should continue or not. The loop will continue to execute the block of code if the **condition** is true.

Here's an example that uses a while loop to print the numbers 1 to 5:

```
int i = 1;
while (i <= 5)
{
    Console.WriteLine(i);
    i++;
}
```

In this example, the **condition** is **i <= 5**, which is true if **i** is less than or equal to 5. The block of code inside the loop will be executed 5 times, with the value of **i** being printed each time.

DO-WHILE LOOPS

A *do-while loop* is like a while loop, except that the block of code is executed at least once before the condition is checked. *The basic structure of a do-while loop is as follows:*

```
do
{
    // block of code to be executed
} while (condition);
```

Here's an example that uses a do-while loop to repeatedly ask the user for a number until they enter a valid number:

```
int number;
do
{
    Console.Write("Enter a number: ");
} while (!int.TryParse(Console.ReadLine(), out number));
```

In this example, the block of code inside the loop prompts the user to enter a number. The **int.TryParse()** method is used to try to parse the user's input as an integer. If the input is not a valid integer, the loop will continue and prompt the user again.

FOR LOOPS

A *for loop* allows you to iterate over a range of values. *The basic structure of a for loop is as follows:*

```
for (initialization; condition; iteration)
{
    // block of code to be executed
}
```

The **initialization** step is used to initialize a variable that will be used to control the loop. The **condition** step is a Boolean expression that determines whether the loop should continue or not. The **iteration** step is used to modify the control variable at the end of each iteration.

Here's an example that uses a for loop to print the even numbers from 0 to 10:

```
for (int i = 0; i <= 10; i += 2)
{
    Console.WriteLine(i);
}
```

In this example, the **initialization** step initializes the variable **i** to 0. The **condition** step checks whether **i** is less than or equal to 10. The **iteration** step increments **i** by 2 at the end of each iteration. The block of code inside the loop will be executed 6 times, with the even numbers from 0 to 10 being printed each time.

BREAKING AND CONTINUING LOOPS

Sometimes you may want to prematurely exit a loop or skip to the next iteration of a loop based on a certain condition. In C#, you can use the **break** and **continue** statements to achieve this.

The **break** statement allows you to exit a loop prematurely. When the **break** statement is executed, the program will immediately exit the loop and continue executing the next statement after the loop.

*Here's an example that uses a while loop with a **break** statement to print the numbers 1 to 5, but exits the loop when the number 3 is printed:*

```
int i = 1;
while (i <= 5)
{
    Console.WriteLine(i);
    if (i == 3)
    {
        break;
    }
    i++;
}
```

In this example, the **if** statement checks whether **i** is equal to 3. If it is, the **break** statement is executed, which exits the loop prematurely.

The **continue** statement allows you to skip to the next iteration of a loop based on a certain condition. When the **continue** statement is executed, the program will skip the rest of the current iteration and start the next iteration.

*Here's an example that uses a for loop with a **continue** statement to print the numbers 1 to 5, but skips the number 3:*

```
for (int i = 1; i <= 5; i++)
{
  if (i == 3)
  {
    continue;
  }
  Console.WriteLine(i);
}
```

In this example, the **if** statement checks whether **i** is equal to 3. If it is, the **continue** statement is executed, which skips the rest of the current iteration and starts the next iteration.

EXERCISE:

1. Write a program that uses a for loop to print the numbers 1 to 10, but only prints the odd numbers.

Use the **continue** statement to skip the even numbers.

CHAPTER 5

ARRAYS AND COLLECTIONS

In programming, an array is a collection of elements of the same data type that are stored in a contiguous block of memory. Arrays are useful for storing and manipulating large amounts of data in a structured way. Collections, on the other hand, are more flexible data structures that can hold elements of different data types.

DECLARING AND INITIALIZING ARRAYS

To declare an array in C#, you need to specify the data type of the array elements, followed by the name of the array and the size of the array in square brackets.

For example, to declare an array of integers with a size of 5, you can use the following code:

```
int[] numbers = new int[5];
```

This declares an array named **numbers** that can hold 5 integers. To initialize the array with specific values, you can use an initializer list enclosed in curly braces.

For example:

```
int[] numbers = new int[] { 1, 2, 3, 4, 5 };
```

This initializes the **numbers** array with the values 1, 2, 3, 4, and 5.

WORKING WITH ARRAY ELEMENTS

You can access individual elements of an array using the index operator (**[]**). The index of the first element in an array is 0, and the index of the last element is the size of the array minus one.

For example:

```
int[] numbers = new int[] { 1, 2, 3, 4, 5 };
Console.WriteLine(numbers[0]); // prints 1
Console.WriteLine(numbers[4]); // prints 5
```

You can also change the value of an element in an array by assigning a new value to the corresponding index. *For example:*

```
int[] numbers = new int[] { 1, 2, 3, 4, 5 };
numbers[2] = 10; // changes the value of the third element to 10
Console.WriteLine(numbers[2]); // prints 10
```

COMMON COLLECTION TYPES IN C#

C# provides several built-in collection types that are more flexible than arrays. *Here are some of the most used collection types:*

- **List<T>:** A dynamic array that can hold elements of any data type. You can add, remove, and modify elements in a List<T> at runtime.

```
List<int> numbers = new List<int>();
numbers.Add(1);
numbers.Add(2);
numbers.Add(3);
Console.WriteLine(numbers[1]); // prints 2
```

- **Dictionary<TKey, TValue>**: A collection of key-value pairs. You can add, remove, and modify elements in a Dictionary<TKey, TValue> at runtime.

```
Dictionary<string, int> ages = new Dictionary<string, int>();
ages.Add("John", 25);
ages.Add("Jane", 30);
Console.WriteLine(ages["John"]); // prints 25
```

- **Queue<T>**: A collection that implements a first-in, first-out (FIFO) policy. You can add elements to the end of a Queue<T> and remove elements from the front of the queue.

```
Queue<string> names = new Queue<string>();
names.Enqueue("John");
names.Enqueue("Jane");
Console.WriteLine(names.Dequeue()); // prints John
```

- **Stack<T>**: A collection that implements a last-in, first-out (LIFO) policy. You can add elements to the top of a Stack<T> and remove elements from the top of the stack.

```
Stack<int> numbers = new Stack<int>();
numbers.Push(1);
numbers.Push(2);
Console.WriteLine(numbers.Pop()); // prints 2
```

EXERCISE:

1. Write a program that uses a List<int> to store a program that uses a List<int> to store a sequence of numbers entered by the user and then calculates the sum of those numbers:

CHAPTER 6

METHODS AND FUNCTIONS

In programming, a method or function is a block of code that performs a specific task. By organizing code into methods or functions, we can break down a large program into smaller, more manageable pieces, and reuse code in different parts of our program.

WHAT ARE METHODS AND FUNCTIONS?

A *method or function* is a named block of code that performs a specific task. Methods and functions can take zero or more input parameters, and may return a value or perform an action.

DECLARING AND CALLING METHODS

In C#, we can declare a method using the following syntax:

```
access_modifier return_type method_name(parameter_list)
{
    // method body
}
```

Here, **access_modifier** is an optional keyword that specifies the visibility of the method (e.g., public, private, etc.), **return_type** is the data type of the value returned by the method (or **void** if the method does not return a value), **method_name** is the name of the method, and **parameter_list** is a comma-separated list of input parameters to the method (or an empty set of parentheses if the method takes no input parameters).

For example, here's a simple method that takes two integer parameters and returns their sum:

```
public int Add(int a, int b)
{
    int sum = a + b;
    return sum;
}
```

To call a method, we use the method name followed by a set of parentheses containing any required input parameters. *For example, to call the **Add** method we defined above, we would write:*

```
int result = Add(3, 4);
```

This would set **result** to **7**, the sum of the two input parameters.

PASSING PARAMETERS TO METHODS

Methods can take zero or more input parameters, which are used to pass data into the method for processing. In C#, input parameters are defined as part of the method declaration inside the parentheses after the method name.

For example, here's a method that takes a string parameter and prints it to the console:

```
public void PrintMessage(string message)
{
    Console.WriteLine(message);
}
```

To call this method and pass in a string parameter, we would write:

```
PrintMessage("Hello, world!");
```

This would print the message "Hello, world!" to the console.

RETURNING VALUES FROM METHODS

Methods can also return a value to the code that called them. In C#, the return type of a method is specified as part of the method declaration. If a method does not return a value, the return type is **void**.

For example, here's a method that takes two integer parameters and returns their sum:

```
public int Add(int a, int b)
{
    int sum = a + b;
    return sum;
}
```

To call this method and get the result, we would write:

```
int result = Add(3, 4);
```

This would set **result** to **7**, the sum of the two input parameters.

EXERCISE:

1. Write a C# method that takes an integer parameter and returns the square of that integer. Then, call the method with an integer input and print the result to the console.

CHAPTER 7

OBJECT-ORIENTED PROGRAMMING

OOP is a programming paradigm that is based on the concept of objects, which can contain data and behaviour. It is one of the most popular paradigms used in software development today.

CLASSES AND OBJECTS

A *class* is a blueprint for creating objects. It defines the attributes and methods that an object of that class will have. An *object* is an instance of a class. It contains the data and methods defined in the class.

Here's an example of a simple class in C#:

```
class Person
{
    public string Name;
    public int Age;

    public void SayHello()
    {
        Console.WriteLine("Hello, my name is " + Name + " and I am " + Age + " years old.");
    }
}
```

In this example, we have a class called **Person**. It has two attributes, **Name** and **Age**, which are of type *string* and *int* respectively. It also has a method called **SayHello** which writes a message to the console using the **Name** and **Age** attributes.

*To create an object of this class, we can use the **new** keyword:*

```
Person john = new Person();
```

This creates a new instance of the **Person** class and assigns it to a variable called **john**. *We can then set the attributes of this object:*

```
john.Name = "John";
john.Age = 25;
```

And call its methods:

```
john.SayHello(); // Output: Hello, my name is John and I am 25 years old.
```

PROPERTIES AND METHODS

In a class, attributes are often referred to as properties, and methods are functions that belong to the class. Properties allow you to encapsulate the data of an object and control access to it. Methods allow you to define the behavior of the object.

Here's an example of a class with properties and methods:

```csharp
class BankAccount
{
    private decimal balance;

    public decimal Balance
    {
        get { return balance; }
        set { balance = value; }
    }

    public void Deposit(decimal amount)
    {
        balance += amount;
    }

    public void Withdraw(decimal amount)
    {
        if (balance >= amount)
        {
            balance -= amount;
        }
        else
        {
            Console.WriteLine("Insufficient funds.");
        }
    }
}
```

In this example, we have a class called **BankAccount**. It has a private attribute called **balance** which can only be accessed through the public property **Balance**. It also has two methods, **Deposit** and **Withdraw**, which modify the **balance** attribute.

Encapsulation refers to the concept of bundling data and methods that operate on that data into a single unit, which is called a class. The purpose of encapsulation is to hide the implementation details of the class from the outside world and to provide a well-defined interface for interacting with the class. In C#, encapsulation is achieved using access modifiers, which control the visibility of members (properties and methods) of a class. There are four access modifiers in C#: public, private, protected, and internal.

- **Public** members are accessible from anywhere, including outside the class.

- **Private** members are only accessible from within the class.

- **Protected** members are accessible from within the class and from derived classes.

- **Internal** members are accessible only from within the same assembly.

It is a good practice to make the fields (variables) of a class private and to provide public properties to access them. This ensures that the class data is protected and can only be accessed through a well-defined interface.

INHERITANCE AND POLYMORPHISM

Inheritance is a mechanism in OOP that allows a class (called a derived class) to inherit properties and methods from another class (called a base class). The derived class can add its own properties and methods, and override or extend the properties and methods of the base class.

Polymorphism is a concept in which objects of different classes can be treated as if they belong to the same class hierarchy. This allows for greater flexibility and extensibility in object-oriented programs.

In C#, inheritance is achieved using the ":" symbol, followed by the name of the base class. For example, the following code defines a derived class called "Employee" that inherits from a base class called "Person":

```csharp
class Person {
    public string Name { get; set; }
    public int Age { get; set; }
}

class Employee : Person {
    public int EmployeeId { get; set; }
}
```

In this example, the **Employee** class inherits the **Name** and **Age** properties from the **Person** class and adds its own **EmployeeId** property.

Polymorphism is achieved through the use of *virtual* and *override* keywords. When a method is marked as virtual in a base class, it can be overridden in a derived class using the override keyword. *For example:*

```csharp
class Animal {
    public virtual void MakeSound() {
        Console.WriteLine("The animal makes a sound");
    }
}

class Dog : Animal {
    public override void MakeSound() {
        Console.WriteLine("The dog barks");
    }
}
```

In this example, the **Animal** class defines a virtual **MakeSound** method, which is overridden in the Dog class to make the dog bark instead of just making a generic animal sound.

EXERCISE:

1. Create a class called "**Shape**" with a method called "**CalculateArea**". Create two derived classes called "**Rectangle**" and "**Circle**" that override the "**CalculateArea**" method to calculate the area of a rectangle and a circle, respectively.

CHAPTER 8

EXCEPTION HANDLING

WHAT ARE EXCEPTIONS?

In programming, an exception is an event that occurs during the execution of a program that disrupts the normal flow of instructions. Exceptions can occur for many reasons, such as invalid input, incorrect usage of a method, or unexpected behavior of an object. When an exception occurs, the program will stop executing unless we handle the exception properly.

TRY-CATCH BLOCKS

A *try-catch block* is a structure in C# that allows us to handle exceptions gracefully. It works by enclosing a block of code that may throw an exception in a try block. If an exception is thrown within the try block, it will be caught and handled by the catch block. The catch block will contain the code to handle the exception, such as displaying an error message or logging the exception details.

Here's an example:

```
try
{
    // code that may throw an exception
}
catch(Exception ex)
{
    // handle the exception here
}
```

In this example, we have a try block that contains the code that may throw an exception. The catch block will catch any exception that occurs within the try block, and the "ex" variable will contain the details of the exception. We can then use this information to handle the exception appropriately.

THROWING EXCEPTIONS

In addition to catching exceptions, we can also throw exceptions manually using the throw keyword. This is useful when we encounter an error that we cannot handle within the current method, and we want to pass the error up the call stack to a higher-level method that can handle it.

Here's an example:

```
if(someCondition)
{
    throw new Exception("Something went wrong!");
}
```

In this example, we are checking a condition, and if it is true, we are throwing a new exception with a message "Something went wrong!". This exception can then be caught and handled by a higher-level method.

EXERCISE:

1. Write a program that takes two numbers as input from the user and divides them. Use a try-catch block to handle any exceptions that may occur during the division. If an exception occurs, display an error message to the user.

CHAPTER 9

FILE I/O AND SERIALIZATION

In this chapter, we will cover the basics of file input/output (I/O) and object serialization in C#. We will learn how to read from and write to files using streams, as well as how to serialize and deserialize objects to and from files.

FILE I/O

File I/O is the process of reading from and writing to files on the disk. In C#, we can use the **FileStream** class to work with files. A **FileStream** object provides a stream for reading or writing data to a file.

To read from a file, we can create a **FileStream** object and use it to read bytes from the file. *For example, the following code reads the contents of a file and prints it to the console:*

```
FileStream fileStream = new FileStream("file.txt", FileMode.Open, FileAccess.Read);
byte[] buffer = new byte[fileStream.Length];
fileStream.Read(buffer, 0, (int)fileStream.Length);
fileStream.Close();
Console.WriteLine(Encoding.ASCII.GetString(buffer));
```

In this example, we create a **FileStream** object for the file "file.txt" with **FileMode.Open** and **FileAccess.Read**, which means we want to open the file for reading. We then create a byte array to hold the contents of the file and call the Read method of the **FileStream** object to read the bytes into the buffer. Finally, we close the **FileStream** object and print the contents of the buffer to the console.

To write to a file, we can create a **FileStream** object and use it to write bytes to the file. *For example, the following code writes a string to a file:*

```
string text = "Hello, world!";
byte[] buffer = Encoding.ASCII.GetBytes(text);
FileStream fileStream = new FileStream("file.txt", FileMode.Create, FileAccess.Write);
fileStream.Write(buffer, 0, buffer.Length);
fileStream.Close();
```

In this example, we create a string and convert it to a byte array using the **Encoding.ASCII.GetBytes** method. We then create a **FileStream** object for the file "*file.txt*" with **FileMode.Create** and **FileAccess.Write**, which means we want to create the file if it does not exist and open it for writing. We then call the Write method of the **FileStream** object to write the bytes to the file. Finally, we close the **FileStream** object.

SERIALIZATION

Serialization refers to the process of converting an object into a stream of bytes that can be stored in a file or sent over a network. Deserialization is the reverse process of converting the bytes back into an object.

Serialization and *deserialization* are useful in scenarios where we need to store objects in a persistent storage or send them over a network. For example, we can serialize an object to a file and then deserialize it later to restore its state.

To serialize an object, we first need to mark it as serializable by applying the **[Serializable]** attribute to its class definition. We can then create a *FileStream* object and pass it to a *BinaryFormatter* object to serialize the object. Here is an example:

```
[Serializable]
class Person
{
    public string Name { get; set; }
    public int Age { get; set; }
}

// Serialize an object to a file
Person person = new Person { Name = "John", Age = 30 };
FileStream fileStream = new FileStream("person.bin", FileMode.Create);
BinaryFormatter formatter = new BinaryFormatter();
formatter.Serialize(fileStream, person);
fileStream.Close();
```

To deserialize the object, we can read the bytes from the file and pass them to the *Deserialize* method of the *BinaryFormatter* object. *Here's an example:*

```
// Deserialize an object from a file
fileStream = new FileStream("person.bin", FileMode.Open);
Person deserializedPerson = (Person)formatter.Deserialize(fileStream);
fileStream.Close();
```

In addition to binary serialization, C# also supports other serialization formats such as XML and JSON. To serialize an object to XML or JSON, we can use the *XmlSerializer* and *JsonSerializer* classes, respectively.

EXERCISE:

1. Create a class **Student** with properties **Name** and **GPA**.

2. Create a list of **Student** objects and add some sample data.

3. Serialize the list to a file using binary serialization.

4. Deserialize the list from the file and print its contents to the console.

CHAPTER 10

BASIC DEBUGGING TECHNIQUES

Debugging is an important skill for any programmer, as it allows you to identify and fix errors in your code. In this chapter, we will cover some basic debugging techniques that can help you track down and fix bugs in your C# programs.

USING BREAKPOINTS

One of the most powerful tools for debugging is the breakpoint. A *breakpoint* is a marker that you can place in your code that tells the debugger to pause execution at that point. This allows you to inspect the state of your program at that point in time and see what is going on.

To set a breakpoint in Visual Studio, simply click in the margin next to the line of code where you want to set the breakpoint. A red dot will appear to indicate that a breakpoint has been set. When you run your program in debug mode, execution will stop at the breakpoint and you can begin inspecting the state of your program.

INSPECTING VARIABLES

When debugging your program, it is often useful to inspect the values of variables at various points in the code. To do this in Visual Studio, you can use the Locals window. This window shows you all the variables that are currently in scope, along with their current values.

To open the Locals window, go to the Debug menu and select Windows > Locals. This will open the window and show you the current state of all the variables in your program. You can also add variables to the watch window, which allows you to monitor the value of a specific variable as your program runs.

DEBUGGING COMMON ERRORS

There are several common errors that can occur in C# programs, such as null reference exceptions, index out of range exceptions, and divide by zero errors. When these errors occur, they can cause your program to crash or behave unpredictably.

To debug these types of errors, it is important to understand what causes them and where they occur in your code. One of the best ways to do this is to use the stack trace, which shows you the sequence of method calls that led up to the error.

In Visual Studio, you can view the stack trace by going to the Debug menu and selecting Windows > Call Stack. This will show you a list of all the methods that were called leading up to the error. By examining the stack trace, you can often identify the source of the error and begin debugging it.

Debugging is an essential skill for any programmer, and by using the techniques covered in this chapter, you can become more effective at finding and fixing bugs in your C# programs. Remember to use breakpoints to pause execution at key points, inspect variables to understand the state of your program, and use the stack trace to identify the source of common errors. With practice, you can become a proficient debugger and write more reliable and robust code.

CONCLUSION

Congratulations on completing this book on C# programming! You have now gained a solid foundation in one of the most popular programming languages used in industry today.

As you move forward in your programming journey, there are still many topics and resources that you can explore to deepen your understanding of C# and expand your skills. Some of these include:

- Advanced topics in OOP, such as interfaces, abstract classes, and delegates.

- Web development with C# using frameworks like ASP.NET.

- Desktop application development with C# using Windows Forms or WPF.

- Game development with C# using game engines like Unity.

- Mobile app development with C# using Xamarin.

- Integration with databases using ADO.NET or Entity Framework.

There are many resources available to help you continue your learning journey, including online tutorials, forums, and books. Some popular resources for C# include:

- Microsoft's official C# documentation and tutorials (https://docs.microsoft.com/en-us/dotnet/csharp/)

- The C# Station (https://www.csharp-station.com/)

- C# Corner (https://www.c-sharpcorner.com/)

- Udemy and Coursera offer online courses on C# programming

With the skills and knowledge you have gained through this book, you are well-positioned for various opportunities in the software development industry. There is a high demand for C# developers, and you can explore job opportunities in fields like web development, game development, desktop application development, and mobile app development.

I wish you all the best in your future endeavours, and I hope that you continue to enjoy programming and learning!

Best regards

KEYWORDS IN C#

- abstract
- as
- base
- bool
- break
- byte
- case
- catch
- char
- checked
- class
- const
- continue
- decimal

- default
- delegate
- do
- double
- else
- enum
- event
- explicit
- extern
- false
- finally
- fixed
- float
- for
- foreach

- goto
- if
- implicit
- in
- int
- interface
- internal
- is
- lock
- long
- namespace
- new
- null
- object
- operator
- out
- override

- params
- private
- protected
- public
- readonly
- ref
- return
- sbyte
- sealed
- short
- sizeof
- stackalloc
- static
- string
- struct
- switch
- this

- throw
- true
- try
- typeof
- uint
- ulong
- unchecked

- unsafe
- ushort
- using
- virtual
- void
- volatile
- while

www.ingramcontent.com/pod-product-compliance
Lightning Source LLC
Chambersburg PA
CBHW081458220526
45466CB00008B/2704